Your Feet Face
FORWARD

An Inspiring Handbook to Life

Colin Wolpert

BALBOA.
PRESS
A DIVISION OF HAY HOUSE

Balboa Press books may be ordered through booksellers or by contacting:

Balboa Press
A Division of Hay House
1663 Liberty Drive
Bloomington, IN 47403
www.balboapress.com
1 (877) 407-4847

Because of the dynamic nature of the Internet, any web addresses or
links contained in this book may have changed since publication and
may no longer be valid. The views expressed in this work are solely those
of the author and do not necessarily reflect the views of the publisher,
and the publisher hereby disclaims any responsibility for them.

The author of this book does not dispense medical advice or prescribe
the use of any technique as a form of treatment for physical, emotional,
or medical problems without the advice of a physician, either directly
or indirectly. The intent of the author is only to offer information
of a general nature to help you in your quest for emotional and
spiritual well-being. In the event you use any of the information in
this book for yourself, which is your constitutional right, the author
and the publisher assume no responsibility for your actions.

Any people depicted in stock imagery provided by Thinkstock are
models, and such images are being used for illustrative purposes only.
Certain stock imagery © Thinkstock.

Print information available on the last page.

ISBN: 978-1-5043-3927-8 (sc)
ISBN: 978-1-5043-3928-5 (e)

Library of Congress Control Number: 2015913665

Balboa Press rev. date: 09/14/2015

Your life is at a crossroad.

In doubt you stand still.
Your head drops forward, your eyes
come to rest upon your feet.
The realization is simple: YOUR FEET FACE FORWARD.
This is the direction in which you must proceed. Go forward.
There is nothing behind you.
Your future begins now.

Contents

Preface ix

Chapter 1 Impermanence.................................. 1
Chapter 2 Western Medicine............................. 3
Chapter 3 Overpaying...................................... 6
Chapter 4 Energy 10
Chapter 5 Reality 14
Chapter 6 Physical Presence 17
Chapter 7 Pain...19
Chapter 8 Yoga..24
Chapter 9 Meditation.....................................28
Chapter 10 Goals and Intentions 34
Chapter 11 Your Now-Life 36
Chapter 12 Deferred Living...............................39
Chapter 13 Congruence and Integrity............... 44
Chapter 14 Distraction.................................... 48
Chapter 15 I Am Not Me..................................50
Chapter 16 Hope is Hopeless 52
Chapter 17 Traffic Lights 55
Chapter 18 Fear of the Fear.............................58
Chapter 19 Timing.. 60
Chapter 20 Destinations...................................63
Chapter 21 Hooks 64
Chapter 22 Difficult Situations......................... 66

Chapter 23 Anger 69
Chapter 24 Gut feeling.......................................70
Chapter 25 Regret...72
Chapter 26 Guilt is Expensive............................75
Chapter 27 Acceptance 76
Chapter 28 The Bow Wave 77
Chapter 29 Beacons..79
Chapter 30 Teaching Yoga 84
Chapter 31 It's Just an Ice Cream. It's Not Forever............ 86
Chapter 32 Trying... 88
Chapter 33 Life Is Important, But It's Not Serious.............. 90
Chapter 34 Life, Death and Grief 92
Chapter 35 Faith.. 94
Chapter 36 Samskaras....................................... 96
Chapter 37 Love.. 98
Chapter 38 The Three People Challenge...................100
Chapter 39 A Second Chance 102
Chapter 40 Shine Alive 103

Preface

One Monday morning I woke up with an idea.

I had figured out a technical solution for reducing the wait that airline reservation agents had to endure when finalizing a guest booking from three minutes down to three seconds.

Off I went and deployed the plan. I felt great.

Later in the day I visited the airline, delaying my ticket to Vancouver so that I could spend a few more weeks in the newly blossoming spring of South Africa. The jasmine fragrances were just too strong to leave behind.

How perfect it all was: green traffic lights, a parking spot in a crowded lot, a three minute line, and my favorite airline lady assisting me. Today, Mmule had a trainee by her side. I spoke to her of letting what comes come and letting what goes go, as I accepted the next perfect date for my travels. Thandi did not understand how life could be so simple and how I trusted the process so easily. I took Thandi's hand, and together we faced the beautiful trees through the window. I asked her to glance down and tell me what she saw. She replied that she saw her feet. I asked, "Where do your feet face?"

Thandi looked at me, and a tear appeared at the window of her soul.

"My feet face forward."

While my technical success of the morning would make a huge difference in many people's lives, it was a drop in the ocean next to Thandi's tear of realization.

My path was now clear: it was to write this book.

With love and light, I wish you the enlightenment of seeing that YOUR FEET FACE FORWARD.

Chapter 1

IMPERMANENCE

I thought my life's work was certain. I loved emergency medicine and had devoted years in service to various hospitals and paramedical organizations. I was bored with university, but it was a means to an end. After all, I had decided this was my path.

Things are often not what they appear to be. In fact, things are seldom ever what they appear to be.

It was a hot, dry day in Africa when my buddy booted up the first 8bit computer I had ever seen. It had a nauseating orange monochromatic screen, no mouse and a clunky keyboard. It was huge, heavy, made odd crunchy noises and beeped a lot. It is true that life surprises us, because mine was never to be the same after this.

I was flummoxed for weeks, figuring out how I was going to buy one of these and what I was going to do with it. As a student, the only way I could afford to buy one was at wholesale prices, so I had no choice but to start a computer company to qualify for this discount. Soon I was supplying computers to all of my friends and their friends. I hired my first employee when I was 20 years old and grew the business for 14 more years. How I ended up in Enterprise Resource Planning & accounting software is a book unto itself.

Working day and night to build a huge enterprise turned out to be an exercise in futility. When work is no longer about survival or creating a comfortable lifestyle, it sometimes becomes a toxic pursuit.

While it may seem obvious to some that we can only wear one pair of shoes at a time, it was a profound realization for me. I found it satisfying and cathartic to give away all but one pair of shoes on that same day that I decided to find a good home for all of my employees and clients, and move on to the next phase of my life.

I no longer felt I needed a fancy two week timeshare if it meant I spent the other 50 weeks working extra hard to pay for it.

When that penny dropped it left a dent in my head.

I spent the next few years working in the African bush among the wild animals. I worked with telecommunications and was infatuated with satellites. In 2005 one of my clients and I sent the very first live video stream of a leopard encounter via an entirely wireless system in a guest chalet.

It was a necessary time in the evolution of my thinking. I was able to just be among nature; a spectator of life. I didn't have to overthink anything. Once the chaos of commerce wasn't driving me, I began to see things with some clarity.

Chapter 2

WESTERN MEDICINE

At the hospital, I lay motionless in the MRI tunnel for three hours. A few weeks before, I was bouncing around the world, cycling, running, swimming and practicing yoga in different cities. I had noticed some tingling in my legs and a constant dull lower back pain, but I was too busy to listen.

The neurologist said he was very sorry about the news, but the pain in my back and numbness in my legs was only going to get worse as the nerve tumor in my lumbar spine, which was already over an inch in diameter, would continue to grow and throttle my nerves.

I was referred to a neurosurgeon who spun a terrifying tale of gloom. He said that I had no other option but to undergo massive spinal surgery, albeit extremely dangerous with a debatable prognosis. The surgery was complicated because many vertebrae in my lower back would have to be cracked open to reach the tumor on the spinal cord. The reconstruction of the spine would involve a significant amount of metal, and of course I would never have flexibility in those areas again.

He told me that regaining sensation in my legs was highly unlikely and that in fact this was the least of my concerns as I was about to lose bladder and bowel control as the tumor grew and constricted the spinal cord.

Recovery from the surgery would take 9-12 months – and a lot of this time would be spent on my back.

The doctor went on to inform me that there was a considerable chance I could I end up worse off after surgery. It was an intricate procedure and sometimes the dissection 'doesn't work out.'

I got a third, fourth and eventually an eleventh medical opinion. I consulted with professors at the university hospital. I was desperate to hear a different answer. Maybe there was a miracle pill or a doctor with a magic wand. I even investigated a radical science-fiction-like device used to blast tumors.

How was this happening to me? What had I done so wrong to have created this bleak situation? Without surgery I was doomed and with surgery I was potentially more doomed.

As children we are taught that doing bad things will result in adverse situations. Accordingly, as adults we perceive that the untoward events in our life are a result of our previous 'bad' actions. The burden of this responsibility weighs on us heavily. We often blame ourselves. While taking responsibility for experiencing the events of our lives is helpful, apportioning sole responsibility to ourselves is incorrect. We do create the events in our lives, but there are seven billion other people simultaneously creating their reality and ours. We create the events in another person's life as much as we create our own.

When we are aligned with universal integrity, the events of our lives are created seemingly more quickly than if we are not – simply because all of the people in the world are creating the same events.

All actions are balanced by reactions. This is the physical law of the universe. What goes up must come down. The reactor pushes into the responder and the result is equal opposite force until the stronger one overcomes. A person who is in pain will do almost anything, whether consciously, subconsciously or spiritually, to ease their pain, and this often has the side-effect of creating pain in the lives of others.

I was completely cornered.

One day in the midst of the panic, it dawned on me that I was rapidly losing traction of the situation and that I had no control anyway. My desperate, reactionary behavior of gripping onto whatever I thought would fix things was actually an exercise in futility. I gave up, surrendering to the fact that I would eventually not be able to walk and I'd be without basic bodily functions. I imagined being this way and totally accepted that if this is what it was going to be – then so be it. I found solace and peace in this place and managed to rest for the first time in a long time.

Chapter 3

OVERPAYING

When you stop interfering with outcomes, by surrendering instead of clinging, and by releasing instead of attaching, you empower yourself with freedom in this moment.

Be prepared to lose everything. Your job, your relationships, your standing in your community, even your existence on this earth. Be willing and prepared to accept losing everything that you are attached to. Nothing is permanent anyway and clinging only makes your life complicated and painful.

I'm not advocating that you actually lose everything. I'm just suggesting that you imagine not having all the things in your life to which you are attached. I'm also not asking you to throw your hands up in defeat and give up. Instead, I'm asking you to be here now and deeply experience your true self without all the attachments in your life.

Practicing this surrender will invite peace into your consciousness, creating freedom and space in the present moment.

Whether the attachment is a valuable piece of jewellery, social status, a job, a lover or a situation – allow all thoughts of attachment to vaporize and realize that you could manage without it. Soon you will discover that the attachment is still there, but you are no longer placing so much importance on having it or needing it to be a certain way. More often than not we create anxiety, stress and pain in the process of desiring something to be a particular way and attempting to influence the outcome.

Clinging to a desired outcome never serves. It only diverts the energy of the situation and creates unnecessary obstacles.

Ask yourself:

How would I be without this thing to which I am so desperately hanging on?

Would my life go on?

Would I really be so much worse off if I didn't get it, or lost it?

What kind of gratitude am I expressing by invalidating what I do have?

What would shift if I simply accepted where I am instead of desiring everything to be different?

Although advancement and improvement are positive things borne of discomfort and a desire for change, this is very different to negating the experience of where you are right now in this moment. You may wish for things to be different in the future, but it is important not to invalidate what you have in this moment right now. This moment is all you have – the next may not come and the past is already gone.

You can be happy with where you are and also seek to have something different in the future.

When you surrender to allowing the next moment or day or week to unfold as it does, while nurturing it with positive intention, you come to see that the moment you are in right now is the present tense of a past moment. Does this give you any more space to simply experience this moment and the next with full engagement, whatever the content? You can change your life in the future, but you owe it to yourself to be present now. How can you enjoy anything if you know that it will eventually end? Would you deny yourself a great meal because you knew it was going to end? Why not engage fully in this moment? Rather than denying the enjoyment of this time, embrace it and its infinite possibilities.

Being present removes the pressure of having to want, which in turn creates freedom and empowers you in the now.

We often endure pain and suffering because we are too scared to rock the boat. We are fearful that if we upset our partner they may leave the relationship. We worry that our boss may fire us and we are anxious that people may think differently of us. So instead, we endure situations that cost us dearly and we overpay to remain in the relationship, job or social circle. We put up with abuse and pain because we are afraid of what we think may be the alternative. We imagine that the only way to reduce pain is to remove the situation and thus we become trapped in our thinking and remain in painful circumstances.

When we realize that it's not the end of the world if we don't have a particular job or relationship, then we have the space to safely explore ways to improve where we are. We have to be prepared to lose it all in order to reach this realization.

Thousands of times a day items are purchased at auctions for much more than they are worth. People are scared of losing, being outbid or simply find themselves automatically reacting and competing for something that they think they want.

No attachment can make you happy or sad. No thing can make you any thing. It is merely the thought of having or not having the attachment that creates emotion. When you cling to the idea of anything, you create fear of losing it. When you accept that attachments are here in the now and may not be in the next moment, then you will find the joy of now. Joy is simply living in the now, whatever it is.

We often assign credibility to the voices of authority and so-called 'reason' inside our heads by accepting that this way is the only way. It seems that we trap ourselves within limited outcome thinking and make broad decisions based on rules that only apply to specific situations.

Once you give yourself permission to leave a situation, you will find the freedom to remain in that space.

Once you give yourself permission to let go, you will find the strength to hold on.

Chapter 4

ENERGY

All actions are energy in motion. Words are energy with sound. There are experiments where scientists subject bodies of water to different sounds and then freeze the water to take photographs of the crystal structures. Beautiful symmetrical patterns develop out of peaceful, joyous harmonics. Loud disturbing sounds create inconsistent disorder.

Newton said for every action there is an equal and opposite reaction. As you stand on the earth, the ground responds with an equal force in the opposite direction. If it didn't, you would crash through the earth. If any one force is stronger than another force, the larger force will overcome the weaker.

The same is true with personalities, emotions, words and thoughts. A strong personality needs to be balanced by another or the weaker personality will capitulate. Not only is this detrimental to the lesser entity, but it also damages the more powerful being because it enables the energy to leak out and free flow without temperance.

Because thoughts are energy in motion, they can easily translate into other forms of energy such as words or actions.

When a thought solidifies it becomes a memory. Traditional belief is that memory is stored in the brain. Every single cell in your body contains the same memory as the next cell. The difference between the brain and any random cell in the body is that the brain is also the main processor of energy exchange. The brain is able to sift through memories and relocate their structures within the body.

A memory originates from thoughts, actions and emotions. When a memory contains more energy than a simple pixel of information, it groups with other similar memories and together they form an e-motion. Energy in motion = e-motion.

Like attracts like. Matter attracts matter. This is a universal truth. The more similar two pieces of matter are, the greater their affinity toward each other.

E-motions affect everything around them and vibrate energy at the particular tone or frequency delineated by their composition. Deep sound is amplified in the belly; high tone is magnified in the head. Each e-motion or group of similar energies that exist together will gravitate toward a particular part of the body.

When e-motions are not free to flow because they are attached to other stagnant emotions, they will settle in specific areas of the physical body until mobilized. If they are not mobilized they will begin to manifest as a lack of congruence in that part of the body, and discomfort will develop. Discomfort causes reaction, usually in the form of movement, which often resolves the blockage. This is why exercise can feel so good and why the body responds positively to it; because the body it is ultimately a temple of moving energy.

Energy resolution can also be achieved through mental processing. Meditation is very powerful.

If we ignore the messages the body is sending us by failing to initiate such shifts, energy will continue to build until injury or illness forces the situation. We set traps for energy by invalidating this information. Sometimes we are so distracted from our bodies that we have no awareness of the warning signs and don't find out about an imbalance until it has become dire. This is when medicine steps in. We can sometimes cut tumors out or heal cancer. But until we resolve the underlying energy leaks and e-motional sources of stagnation, the tumor, illness or injury will return.

It is widely believed that anger resides in the liver. What happens when an angry person hurts another by way of words, actions or thoughts? Does this resolve the anger stored in the liver? Yes and no. Yes, it gets some angry energy out. But does it dissolve the anger? No. Does it transfer the anger to the next person? Absolutely. Being angry at the world hurts others.

There has to be an equal and opposite reaction. Either someone will take on that anger and ultimately retransmit it, or it can be met with an equal and opposite amount of love, which will neutralize the energy. There is an infinite amount of love in this universe. A tear of anger doesn't last long in the ocean of love.

This is why love is the answer to everything. Not romantic, happy love, but love as the universal entity. Love that is life, love that is you, me, everything that is and will be. If you realize that you are only passing through this state of humanness as an expression of the existence of love, you will have no option but to abandon all ego and live your life in a loving state.

Chapter 5

REALITY

During my high school and university years, I worked as a volunteer medic at numerous hospitals, clinics and fire stations in Southern Africa. For five years I spent 40 hours per week in public service instead of hanging out with my peers at parties and nightclubs. I missed out on many youthful pastimes, yet I would unequivocally choose this path again.

I learned so much that had absolutely nothing to do with medicine in the emergency room. I loved my weekend shifts in the huge government hospitals. Outside of this, some of my favorite times were vaccinating children in rural clinics where we collected water in buckets from the river to wash hands between patients. I wasn't particularly fond of travelling at high speed in the paramedic response vehicles, but I quickly learned how to maintain composure in frantic situations.

No lesson that we learn is ever wasted. Situations that require these skills will present themselves in time. The existence of tumultuous and challenging circumstances in this moment creates our future capabilities and aptitude.

It was in these early days that I began to realize the simplicity of life. You are born, you live, you die – everything else is purely a bonus and the only pity is not to embrace every second and every moment, whatever the content.

When I surrendered to my tumor situation as being simply what it was, an unimaginable lucidity overcame me. I became able to let thing be as they were.

I realized that this was only an event in my life, somewhere between birth and death. How it turns out will simply be how it turns out. When we start to negotiate with how we think our lives should be in the next moment as opposed to how our lives are in the current moment, this is when we create anguish and anxiety.

I'm not advocating a nihilistic inattention to your life. Instead, nurture your dreams, honor your destinations and meet your obligations – without the associated angst of clinging to outcomes and results.

We cannot reverse into the past, and even if we could, we are not qualified to decipher what was for the greater good and what wasn't. What appears in our interpretation as something untoward may be fertile garden for something else.

Accepting responsibility for your situation and taking deliberate action to express your life with wholesome intention is empowering and valuable. If you choose to accept any obligation – let it be to honor the life force within you by validating your own presence in the now.

When a leaf on a tree is diseased, it doesn't mean that the whole tree should be written off. Even if a body is completely riddled with cancer – this doesn't invalidate the life force that still resides within it. Too often we make decisions outside the scope of our understanding and perceive black or white as the only options.

Giving up doesn't mean abandoning your desire for life, nor does it imply defeat. Giving up is about surrendering to the outcome of the story while maintaining positive intention and being actively committed to engaging the processes of life as they unfold.

Chapter 6

PHYSICAL PRESENCE

If you're seeking spirituality outside of yourself, you may be wasting your time.

You are a spiritual being that exists in your physical body in order to experience your essence. The more physically present you are, the more you will experience your spirituality.

You are never anywhere else except right here, right now. To seek spirituality is to look in the mirror and miss seeing yourself exactly where you are.

With this in mind, we can understand our manifestation into human form for a period of time. When your physical body dies, maybe you go back to where you came from and the cycle completes - or maybe it continues. It's really not important to know this – it shouldn't make any difference to how we live. If there are consequences to your life once it is over, would you do anything differently? If you would, why aren't you doing it right now?

We will never be able to understand where we were before we were here - because the only answer is that we were in the place that we were before we were here.

As spirit we experience everything; as humans we experience humanness. Why are you alive as human and not alive as a bird in the sky? Whatever you believe about your creators, the same life force that flows through the lungs of a cow flows through your every cell.

The essence of your life is simple—it's spiritual. You have no need to chase it or look for it anywhere. That is not the point, purpose or requirement of this life. All beings are spiritual - as are the trees, rivers, animals, planets and the universe. The manifestation of your spirituality is in your physical being. The tail-chasing exercise of finding oneself through spirituality can never yield a result. Connecting, really deeply connecting with your physical self, is the only way that you will ever come to experience your truth and your spiritual existence. It is in this place that you will feel that you are not an indivisible part of the whole. Instead, you are the whole.

Chapter 7

PAIN

Physical and emotional pain is the quickest, most effective way to experience being deeply present in the now. You are always right here, right now when you are in pain.

My physical pain was insignificant compared to the emotional anguish consuming me. Would committing to this surgery and months of physical therapy be the solution, or would I end up worse off? The echo of doom from that first neurosurgeon reverberated in my head like a jackhammer. His words constantly plagued me.

The persistent dull pain gnawing at my nerves was feeding my fear, anguish and worry. There is no doubt that I preferred short, sharp, stabbing bursts of pain to less intense relentless throbbing. Yet how was I going to absorb the intelligence that this deep pain was seeking to share with me if I was easily able to forget it during moments of reprieve?

The only way I was ever going to hear anything was when I started to pay appropriate attention to the pain. Habitually reverting to replaying old mental movies and keeping repetitive thoughts is not possible when pain is constant.

Pain is here to talk to us – it is in fact a gift. When we don't listen to the gentle messages being offered to us, they have no option but to begin screaming at us. If we still ignore this, then illness and disease will manifest.

Being physically confined to bed and severely restricted in my movement, my life was reduced to a sober existence. The emotional pain of not being on my yoga mat daily and maybe never being on my mat again was petrifying. How scary would my life be if I could never practice yoga again? In retrospect, my yoga practice was an attachment. Certainly some attachments are valuable – the trick is not to cling to their presence or want them to be different from how they are, as this is the cause of suffering.

I knew that if I could get back on the yoga mat and move, some of the pain would soften and my mood would lift. But this seemed impossible. It was a vicious cycle.

I learned a trick in the times that I was feeling ok. I reminded myself of how badly I had felt a little while before. Then I deliberately took note of how good I was feeling in the present moment and figured out a way to remember that feeling in the future for the inevitable return of the pain. I used to wrap my meditation beads around my wrist and wear them like a bracelet when I was feeling strong and happy. When the bad times arrived I would see the beads on my hand and it would remind me that I had been in a good place before and would be in a good place again soon.

Being prepared to lose it all includes giving up the difficult times too. Clinging to difficulty is a human habit – we are averse to letting things go, whatever they are. But the same freedom that is gained by releasing things that don't serve us is also the empowerment that allows us to release difficulty and gain neutrality, ultimately finding a place of stillness.

Being unable to practice hatha (movement based) yoga, I decided to find some alternate yoga sequences that didn't involve my lumbar spine. I met with my yoga teacher and took the MRI scans along to illustrate the obstacle.

What began as a quest to find some different yoga options turned into a life-altering experience. My teacher looked deeply into my eyes and with a soft, gentle voice reminded me that all the tools needed to help myself were already inside of me. She suggested that I drink copious amounts of a vegetable juice concoction, meditate and chant. It was a very matter of fact kind of discussion lasting only a few minutes.

I've always believed that illness and physical manifestation of disease develop energetically in the mind – but for some ridiculous reason I had panicked and discarded this belief, instead collapsing as a victim into the net of traditional medical doctrine that renders the patient powerless.

The next moment in my life was a blissful reawakening to the innate knowledge inside of me. It wasn't good enough to just hear what the pain was telling me – I had to realign my existence by healing. It was my responsibility to restore my body back to maximum health. It was my obligation to all who loved me.

After all, if I had created this untoward situation, I was capable of choosing to create a positive outcome.

I firmly believe that this path would not have unfolded in the way it did, had I not decided a few days before to take my chances with surgery. Not only had I surrendered to maybe never recovering, I had also surrendered one step further to possibly being even worse off after surgery. Despite the emotions, I remained optimistic and deep down I knew that everything was going to be ok – I just didn't have a clue as to how it was going to happen.

I really wasn't looking for a solution anymore. I had resigned myself to the fact that the surgery was the only choice, and I was going to take my chances. The pain was not getting any better each day – not at all.

The reality of severe physical pain is that it can be numbed with pills, but this has the side-effect of disconnecting the mind from the body and thereby detaching the whole from source. I refused any sort of painkiller.

There are only ever two options when dealing with pain. Either we listen to the messages that the pain is delivering or we suffer.

Many great teachers remind us that pain is inevitable, yet suffering is optional. Suffering is entirely a cognitive decision. Choices are merely thoughts and thoughts are completely within our control. This moment provides the opportunity to cease playing your pain story over and over. This moment offers the space to be free from the shackles of suffering. It's just a choice.

There is no point in drudging up past pain.

Pain Exercise:

Remind yourself that the pain you feel is only what you have assigned to a situation or event. An event contains no pain or pleasure.

1. What is paining you?
2. When did you last feel this way?
3. How did this pain in the past define an aspect of you?
4. How does this pain lead you away from your core happiness now?
5. What behavior do you exhibit or find yourself playing out to avoid this particular pain?
6. Whose fault is it?
7. Why are they wrong?
8. What would fix it?
9. Assume that your pain is a cloud with a silver lining. What is the positive side and result?

Repeat the above process until no more answers come. Then leave it alone and forget about it. It will heal itself after a few sleeps.

Chapter 8

YOGA

"If you always do what you've always done, you'll always get what you've always got." – Henry Ford

About a year before the tumor was discovered, I had found yoga. The gym offered yoga classes as a group fitness activity a few times per week.

What I found on the mat was something amazing that I had never experienced before. There was a calm that engulfed me each time I rolled out my mat, followed by space in my head and in my life.

I'm not being abstract or speaking in metaphor. Spending time on a yoga mat offers subtle lessons about things that you didn't know that you didn't know. What happens on the mat literally happens in your life. When you breathe through challenges, you learn that skill for future use off the mat. When you get annoyed and restless, instead of rolling up the mat and going home, you realize that you do have a choice to stay a while longer and witness the discomfort passing. In time the habits of the mat seep into your life.

Yoga is most powerful in that we use all the tools we have to get into a particular shape and keep doing that until one day we discover that we can achieve the same thing using a different method, or more importantly, that the destination isn't the point. Instead there is another space, very similar, yet a very different place to find one's self. If it weren't for yoga's liberating effect on my mind and its ability to create newfound flexibility, I may have completely missed the alternate options and ended up being chopped up by the neurosurgeon.

Our brains are not programmed to proactively seek new ways to achieve old goals. Once we know how to do something, our habit is to take that ability for granted and we seldom question the way in which it is performed. Accordingly, when we have a monumental, unexpected problem, it seems the only quest is for a solution. In fact, the framing of an obstacle as a problem forces us into a processing mode that diminishes our choice to a limited, outcome-seeking solution.

Is the obstacle in your path indicative or informative? By asking yourself whether the kink in your process is to advise you of something or to interrupt your advance, you are able to proceed. The light bulb wasn't invented in linear process. There were many pieces of information that sculpted the thinking in order to develop a path to the solution. The final result was not an intention at the start – it was an idea that developed by keen observation of the feedback at each step. It's important not to become fixated on an outcome, because most likely the end result will be better than you expected if you surrender to the process and pay attention.

Being so bent on reaching specific destinations, we often miss out on the variability along the way. As habit, we perceive twists in the road as obstacles instead of indicators.

All I wanted was to get out of the situation. The only way to achieve this seemed to be finding a fix and getting to the destination as quickly as possible, with little distraction. I had no other options in my head and no space to consider half-measures or partial recovery. I was hell bent on the endgame and it was black or white.

When a car has a flat tire, our immediate response is to fix the situation by changing to the spare or fixing the flat. It's about getting going again. It's never about stopping to see where we are and pausing for a moment to listen to our universe. The car has a flat anyway – whether we experience this moment or rush on to the next will not alter the situation. We are constantly rushing to get somewhere and hardly ever experience the journey - certainly not the paused journey. It is the pauses that define your life.

Instead of learning to deal with uncomfortable situations and empower ourselves to frame these events as positive growth experiences, we react in the same way time after time and are surprised because we were expecting a different result this time around. If you plant a tree, a fish is not going to grow out of the earth. Yet we continue to repeat the same patterns and expect different result in our lives. When that doesn't happen, our next natural response is to remove the situation. Anyone can deal with a crisis by reacting. It takes courage to stand still and experience what life is offering. It takes real courage to give up the idea of a something altogether, let alone to re-invent it.

When your life is ready for yoga, meditation or any of the wisdom practices, or when it's time to expand your practice, the clues will appear. Maybe this realization will be in the distant future or maybe this is why you came to read this book, right here, right now. You don't have to wait for disaster– you can choose to make conscious decisions in your life right now. Your life is not a telephone waiting for someone to call.

Once a heart is liberated, it will shine alive. I truly believe that this is why millions of people are devoted to the practice of yoga.

On the days when I am resistant to my practice, I go anyway because there is a class full of yogis waiting to exchange energy. Good energy from one person is ten thousand times more powerful than bad energy from ten thousand people.

Chapter 9

MEDITATION

Giving is the best feeling in the world. Refusing to accept something from someone, be it a gift, love, care or teaching is not only a disservice to one's self - it is denying that person the joy of giving. Learning to receive is the greatest gift with which we can honor ourselves and others. In receiving we are in fact giving.

For years I dabbled unsuccessfully with attempts at sitting still and closing my eyes in order to meditate. Then an inspiring Buddhist nun introduced me to another kind of meditation that is practiced with open eyes and specifically encourages the use of the senses in order to anchor one's self in the moment. In what seemed like a comedy of coincidences, I attended a weekend workshop at a local yoga studio, which just goes to show how the simplest of intentions put into motion by one person can change a life forever. Of course, at the time I had no idea that this workshop was going to offer me some of the valuable tools that ultimately contributed to me being able to travel this road and be here now.

My yoga teacher had included meditations in my daily work and I began each day with these. The first few days were challenging, but after I found a traditional little wooden bench, it became much easier.

I practiced every day for hours, working through the yoga kriyas – meditating, chanting, moving and visualizing. Traditional visualization is described as creating as opposed to de-creating. Things can't be de-created. We can only work toward creatively facilitating the transformation of things.

This is how I began the work. I realized that I had to draw from everything else in my life that was in harmony. To concentrate on everything that was good and aligned would overwhelm the tumor. The process of visualizing was not focused on reducing the tumor, but rather on amplifying everything around it that was wholesome and aligned, until the tumor had no space to exist. The process of creating happiness in your life is not by removing the sadness; it is by being grateful for the good and focusing on everything joyous.

We create harmony which is in alignment with the integrity of the universe. This is a place where there is order and custom, the laws of physics govern and there are no maverick tumors that appear by chance. The universe exists in alignment with the rules that have created life itself. It is from the universe that life evolved and from life that the universe creates.

Effective visualization is a present tense activity focused on process, whereas deferred thinking is an escapist exercise in fantastical daydreams. Imagining the tumor gone would not be effective as a process to remove it – that would be expecting some magic wand to do the work, when instead the deep lessons from the process needed to be imbibed in order to heal. Why else would these tremendous obstacles be created if not to fully learn from the lesson?

The very nature of our universe is based upon growth from small to large. There are no clouds of smoke that manifest large objects from nothing. Everything has to start somewhere and grow. We don't attend school just to get a certificate. We absorb the knowledge via a path of learning so as to hold the intelligence meaningfully. If tumors could come and go at whim, it would be no different to blinking the eyelids; an inert experience that teaches no lessons or imparts no knowledge. Embracing the process of all that is, is the essence of life. No shortcuts, no long detours; simple presence in the now as it is.

When I refer to the universe, it's not an abstract way of referring to something else – it's the universe; the place where the stars and sun and planets live. Some may have spiritual connotations and special words for this – I prefer not to hold affiliation to words or labels that seek to define it. Religion has no place in yoga. While some people may perceive similarities, any attempt to tie these completely different concepts together only causes confusion. Yoga is yoga, religion is religion, a sauna is a hot place and sitting in the sun is also hot.

Music is no different to light. It gets concentrated into bands of existence and sounds a particular way because there is more of one frequency than the rest of the ambient sound. All the colors together appear as white light. Scientists explain that when you see a colored object, you are actually seeing that particular color reflected because all the other component colors of white light are absorbed by the object.

It is said that if we could hear the sound of the conglomerate universe it would sound like the 'om' that is often sung by spiritualists. Chanting this sound doesn't mean anything – it is a musical note that sounds like the universe and to chant it is to resonate at this vibration in unison with all else in existence. When you meditate or chant to the sound of 'om', you are connecting to everything that is universally aligned. When you concentrate on healing something, you are in fact focusing on everything else except the illness, disease or pathology. The way to empower the wisdom of universal healing is to concentrate on everything that is good and universally aligned, excluding the pathology.

Traditional medicine seeks to treat the illness or disease by targeting it. Universal healing concentrates on everything except the illness or disease. Sometimes we need a combination.

Soon the MRI scans became crystal clear in my mind, and after a few days I was able to locate and envisage the tumor in my spine. The emotions I felt were akin to the coming home of a long lost friend whom I loved profoundly. It wasn't enough to logically visualize my spine. Instead there was a triangulated connection shared between head, heart and spine.

By concentrating on all that was good and right around the tumor, each day I would envisage it shrinking. After all, a lotus flower grows out of muddy, dirty water. Every day I became more and more connected to the tumor and I started to understand what it was doing in my body, why it was there and what message it had come to share with me.

Day after day I meditated and did the work. A few days before I was scheduled for surgery I went for another MRI scan, this time to establish a baseline from which the neurosurgeon could work.

Imagine my surprise in discovering that the tumor was a smidgen smaller since the prior scan a few weeks before. How was this possible? What had caused this? It wasn't medication, because I wasn't taking any. Nor was it chemotherapy or radiation, because I hadn't had any.

Was it maybe the juice, the meditation, the yoga and the positive outlook? Could it be?

This was the brightest green traffic light I had ever seen. It was a crystal clear message to stay on this road, to keep at it, to persevere and not to give in. In retrospect that moment was one of the first few steps that lead me to immerse myself into the healing practice of self-care and love using the modality of yoga.

It was a negotiation each day. If I listened attentively and imbibed the messages, I was able to reduce the size of the tumor. Some days I would get over-zealous and want more to dissolve away, but this didn't work. I'd push for the imaginary picture of the MRI in my head to have a smaller dent in my spine and it just wouldn't. Only a smidgen of a millimeter of healing would transpire each day because I needed to understand every message in a crystal clear context.

From my days in the medical world I remembered the doctors telling parents that it takes as long for kids to heal as it does for them to get sick. This was usually in the context of measles and mumps and childhood afflictions. This bit of information was an anchor for me, enabling me to trust the process. I figured that as long as I was doing the work, the healing would happen and it didn't matter how long it was going to take or how long it had taken to get here in the first place. As long as I had halted the destructive cycle and was moving towards health, all was good.

There is so much truth in the saying that the longest journey is begun by taking the first step. You don't need to see the end right now or even know what it might look like.

Chapter 10

GOALS AND INTENTIONS

Too often we abandon the journey because we think that the destination is unreachable. We set goals instead of intentions. With intentions we are free to move the goal posts and allow constantly evolving situations to serve us in the highest manner.

Goals don't allow this freedom because they are specific and unforgiving. The person with an intention to win a marathon will train as hard as the person with a goal to do the same. The difference is that the person with intention can never fail, but has a perfectly good lottery ticket that is self-compassionate, self-rewarding and self-loving.

Swimming is one of the best exercises for spinal conditions. It relieves the pressure of gravity and allows fluid movement and flexion. I used to set goals of swimming 100 laps in an hour. Some days I managed. Others I finished a few short. On the days when I didn't make the 100, I was disappointed and self-critical, invalidating the 98 lengths that I had swum. Yet when I changed my intention - to swim as many laps as I could in an hour - I often exceeded the 100. On the days when I didn't,

I was still successful because I showed up, exercised and felt wonderful from the breathing.

Intention holds the gift of self-compassion. If you can be kinder to yourself, you are infinitely more caring towards the world, which ultimately is the joy around you that dissolves anything untoward in yourself. If you set yourself up for success with intentions, you will most probably exceed any goals that you may have pegged in the sand.

In my journey as a yogi, I've since discovered myriads of meditation techniques. Each and every technique has a place, catering to different constitutions. All meditation shares a common simplicity – be here, in the now.

When you meditate, you open your life up to receiving details of the clues which expose secrets of infinite possibility. Without any effort, you allow universal knowledge to permeate your being and program your consciousness.

Allowing your mind to be free of clutter and accepting that this moment is perfect as it is will foster an environment conducive to meditation.

As soon as you surrender and stop yearning to change anything in this moment, instead embracing the now as it is, the sooner you will create the space to manifest the next moment with clarity and purpose.

Chapter 11

YOUR NOW-LIFE

Pain and suffering is perceived when what we think we want differs to what is actually happening in our lives.

The idea that we are born perfect, somehow become flawed and then need to heal in order to return to baby-like perfection is awry. In fact, it's completely ridiculous - we are born perfect and remain perfect.

Any belief that things should be different to how they are is only thought playing out in our ego. We buy into the lie that things are not perfect and then we pain ourselves over finding ways to 'heal' in order to get back to so-called innocent perfection.

It's usually when we're in a place of disappointment and pain that we allow our minds to create fantasies of being elsewhere. It's a natural response to make things feel better. We believe that we can't change what is, so we fantasize about what the future could be. Whether you're living in the moment or imaging yourself in another moment, it's the same thing to the brain.

Every living organism's natural response to pain or discomfort is to avoid it at all costs. When we find ourselves in situations that are not pleasing, we calculate ways to get out of them. We construct elaborate schemes to ease the pain and tell ourselves stories about how it could be different. Then we imagine ourselves inside of these fantasies, and this feels a lot better than the unpleasant situation.

Once we have the next fantasy, we embark on the journey of chasing it. What invariably happens is that somewhere down the line we realize that we are nowhere near the fantasy destination. This creates even more pain because the distance to the fantasy is more evident. And so we embark on a new fantasy to replace the old fantasy, which just leads to the next disappointment, time after time.

The road that your life follows has very little to do with you as an individual. The path you choose to travel and the events along the way are indicative of whether you are listening to universal air traffic control or not. If you aren't on your right path, things won't work until you get onto it. The further you stray from your right path, the louder the messages have to be in order to get you there.

When life flows and happens with ease, then you are on the correct path.

The events on the path of your life are result of the choices you make. You may wonder- how does this explain something like the illness of a child, or a stillborn baby – how could that child have chosen this? Who experiences the death of the child? Certainly the child – but also all the people around the child who have a vested interest, and all the other children in the world who will survive because this child didn't. Knowledge will be gained from the lesson of this child's death. There will be repercussions in the world.

All birth will end in death, all pain and suffering will end in peace – it's just the amount of time between the beginning and end that varies. Getting stuck on why and how will only prolong the time you spend in pain. Life happens this way and we can choose to experience the moment instead of attaching to the pain of the past. Severe pain in a moment passes – in that moment only a portion of the pain is actually felt. It is only in the next moments when we replay the event in our minds and make decisions about the memory and the outcome - about how terrible it was and how we will languish in the space of sadness - that pain becomes unmanageable.

Chapter 12

DEFERRED LIVING

The state of living in a fantastical world where things are different to how they actually are is called 'deferred living'. We talk about the next great holiday, the next job, the next relationship. We invalidate the present because we are thinking about the next thing.

Deferred living is about avoiding where we are now, and it becomes a pattern and a habit. Even when we are totally content in the moment, our brains are so stuck in 'the next' that we often miss out on experiencing our NOW-LIFE.

In addition to deferring our NOW-LIFE to the future, we often live in a pending or de-pending state. We postulate that when this happens, then that will be true. If only I could win the lottery, equates to 'until I win the lottery, my life remains 'pending' and I give away my power and withhold my permission to express joy in this moment'.

The result of this is that we think we are not happy because we don't have what we want. This implies that we cannot be happy until we have it. What we must accept is that we already have the perfect circumstance right now in this moment. It doesn't need to be more or different. It may transpire that in time we will have more of our desired attachments, but this is not the point of life. It detracts from the point of being. In this moment we have the perfect circumstance and the perfect life. When we take responsibility and see that the life we are living in this moment is a result of what we have created for ourselves, then we give ourselves space and permission to exist in the present and not fantasize and negotiate with ourselves about the future.

When we realize that the wonderful circumstances in our lives are a result of our allowing them to be created, then we can be kind to ourselves and grateful for our power to manifest. The other side of this coin is blaming ourselves for the negative content of our lives. When things are not going as we wish them to, the mind spends time negotiating with the obstacles instead of focusing on the positive. This causes the creation of negativity, which interferes with the process that manifests the next positive event in our lives.

Our thoughts are the seeds of the events in our lives. Your conscious thoughts feed the subconscious mind, which amplifies these intentions. To break the cycle of negativity, change the thought by shifting the focus. Concentrate on the positive in your life. You can squeeze the negativity out of your life by accepting that all of the events in your life are positive and in alignment with universal existence.

The homeostasis that exists as the manifestation of our lives is easily susceptible to the momentum of our thoughts. Have you ever heard the negative exclamation of 'I knew this would happen to me!'? Life may have been proceeding perfectly well up to that point. Then something less pleasing occurs, just as expected and created. What's the payoff? Is it so that you can be 'right' about expecting disaster by cultivating negative thoughts? Why make yourself suffer so that you can be right?

If you shroud your thoughts with sub-surface negativity, this will erode the positivity in your life. It's so easy to promulgate the negatives in life, slipping into a false narration. "This is wrong, that is bad, this disaster, that crisis". It's all just thoughts culminating in sharp hooks that we lunge towards and bite hard onto. It's easy to drop into this space when we are not paying attention. It takes work to be fully present and consciously nurture positivity. How can we serve ourselves or others in any way if we dissolve the wonderful joy that is so precious amid the chaos of the world?

If you decide that the negativity in your life doesn't serve you and really doesn't need to exist, you will give yourself permission to create the freedom and space to think happy, positive thoughts and live a deliberate, intentional life.

During the time of my healing, I was often challenged in explaining why I might have created this difficult and negative event. This sort of question is natural, but in fact the correct question is: what purpose does this obstacle have in my life, how is it serving me, everyone around me and the world? Most importantly, why do I perceive this situation as bad? Everything in life is for the good – the universe tends toward a higher plane of existence. We can ask ourselves: how can I seek to be grateful for the circumstances around this seemingly devastating event rather than fixating on the negativity?

It is what it is.

Our natural instinct to understand why things are the way they are in order to justify them can never be satisfied. The path you travel is a narrow band on the wide road of life. The choices you make allow you to meander in slight deviations – but you will always remain on the road. The road is the road. The choices that you make define your experience of the scenery and events along the way.

The momentum and flow of the world imposes a force that causes us to move and be a part of it all. If you were to stop suddenly, you would be bumped. Life's tendency is to vacillate and breathe. It is identical to the universal physical laws of nature. Stars wobble in their orbits and everything is constantly contracting and expanding. The moon affects massive bodies of water and creates ocean tides, yet the oceans exert force on the moon and cause it to wobble.

Your path is a narrow track defined by a few footprints among billions. There are no footprints ahead of you. No one has ever travelled the exact path that lies before you. Some people may have had similar experiences, but the same experience has different purpose for different people. Dropping an ice cream on the road may be devastating to a child, but the experience for you may be an opportunity to be kind by preventing the couple behind you from slipping on the ice cream. The traffic on any road is your fellow beings living alongside you – you have as much right to be there as they do and they have as much right as you.

The story telling part of the brain is unable to distinguish between reality and fiction, so it keeps us placated by playing the same "ideal" fairy tale story over and over. It's no surprise that the mind will avoid 'the now' at all costs when it can be so easily distracted by fantasy.

Because we perceive that we are not living in our fantasy, we take our thoughts back to the original fiction again and again. This perpetuates the loss cycle. We create a new fantasy because we "failed" at the old fantasy. Even if you are to obtain everything within your fantasy, you will simply create another, and the process will keep repeating itself until one day you wish that you were back at the beginning – a newly born infant starting again with a fresh slate. You don't need to start again. Each moment is a beginning. A simple choice to take a deep breath and begin is all that it takes to live in your NOW-LIFE.

Chapter 13

CONGRUENCE AND INTEGRITY

Congruence manifests when the facets of the self are operating together in alignment. When we are living an authentic life by maintaining congruence between our thoughts, actions and words, we are empowered to manifest circumstances that support our lives. Everything we need will be present without any effort.

Integrity refers to our capacity to resonate with the universe around us.

You cannot exist in a high state of integrity and a low level of congruence. To be aligned with the universe and therefore exist in integrity with it, one has to be congruent within the self first. Your level of congruence resonates outward and causes attraction to beings and situations that exist in a similar state. The more disconnected the relationship between the aspects of your self, the lower your level of integrity and connection with the universal momentum of life. By believing in what you say and acting accordingly, you will create situations and events as you wish them to be.

Life exists perfectly. It is an exercise in futility to believe that we can fight the way the universe exists by operating by rules that are not of universal service to all.

If you commit to doing something, do it. If you are not intent on taking a particular action, maintain the congruence in your speech by saying so. Once you have committed to doing something, inaction thereafter is inconsistency that will disrupt the harmony and integrity in your life.

Being true to your self and simultaneously choosing not to take action is a perfectly acceptable decision. Yet we often agree to things that don't serve us. This festers within, causing discord our lives. Even if your decision isn't popular, as long as you are being congruent and therefore remaining in integrity, it will always yield positivity.

If you strike a tuning fork in a room, any other tuning forks in the room will all start to vibrate and resonate at the same frequency. This happens without any physical contact between them. And so it is true of our bodies and our thoughts. The force of energy that we exude causes the things around us to take on the same characteristics.

Integrity is found in the connection between self and everything else in the universe.

When there is congruence between your thoughts, words and actions, you will automatically be in integrity with everything around you. As you practice self-truth, the people, events and landscapes around you change. A drop of water cannot exist alone in an ocean.

Some cities will feel better to you than others, some landscapes and oceans more attractive. Different people will feel better to be around than others. The closer you come to congruence and integrity, the more peaceful the world will feel.

If you are thinking one way and acting in a different way, it's literally a tug of war between your truth and your toes. This is how we often create events and circumstances in our lives that are similar to our intentions – but not quite. It also explains how we sometimes create situations that are not similar to our wishes at all. We will always create external events that match the level of congruence inside of us. If we are operating from an internal place of inconsistency, the external world will mirror this.

When you find that your actions and speech do not match your thoughts, this is indicative that something needs to change. If you're faking it, your subconscious knows this and creates a cesspool of incongruence. We cannot expect to bring about events in our lives that fall into perfect place when our conscious minds are busy invalidating and suppressing thoughts. All this does is create disparity between the conscious and subconscious mind. The world outside is always a reflection of the world inside.

When we label what is present in our lives as not being what we want, then we invite disappointment to permeate our thoughts and ultimately invalidate ourselves. This feeds our subconscious, which keeps hearing 'this is not what I want, I want something else'. When an experience is perceived as bad, we get more desperate and more upset and wish that our lives could be different. This blocks us from manifesting our conscious truths, as the congruencies in our brain are being negatively influenced by a lack of gratitude.

When we accept the circumstances of our lives, we dissolve conflicting thoughts. Then we can begin to manifest fulfillment.

The process of influencing our subconscious minds to be aligned with our conscious thoughts is facilitated through the practices of humility, acceptance and gratitude. Gratitude is precursory to love and joy.

Once you acknowledge that every circumstance in your life was co-created by you, you will begin to see your power to harness manifestation. Limited congruence will only manifest events of limited congruence. Truth manifests meaningful abundance.

Chapter 14

DISTRACTION

When you look for nothing, you will find everything.

Being present and really experiencing your life is not always a rose garden. Life can be thorny.

What is life anyway? If it is not being here and experiencing this very moment, the alternative is your "not-now life," also known as your "distracted life."

When we can't bear to be in the moment, we distract ourselves. The more we distract ourselves, the more distractions we need.

For example, you're having a difficult day, so you go for a run. You start out slowly, but gradually increase the pace because the distraction isn't strong enough to keep you distracted. Running is hard and you need a distraction from the distraction, so you go faster. But running faster is even more difficult, so you add another distraction: music and headphones. Eventually the distraction from the distraction leads to destruction, typically a physical injury.

Ironically, being in the original moment was more peaceful and endurable than the ultimate destruction. If you don't stop to take stock and return to basics, life eventually becomes the distraction from the distraction. You end up where you started, but maybe with a physical injury to keep you in "the now."

An injury will always take you to the beginning of a path that you need to walk. The more distracted you are, the more dramatic the injury will be.

We cannot ignore parts of ourselves. We have brains and emotions. This is no accident. Anyone who says that you should listen solely to your heart and ignore your gut feelings and thoughts is mistaken. You are here to find congruence between your heart and head — not to ignore one or the other.

Your body, mind and heart are the physical manifestations of the work you are here to do. The circumstances in which you exist provide the nourishment and seeds to accomplish this. There is no good, no bad — only decisions and interpretations based on comparison and judgement. Some people have it "easier" or "harder" than other people — that is the nature of life. It is not our place to judge. It is our work to be everything we can be by being present in our own lives.

You can go through life in one of two ways. The first is to be present and experience your stuff as you work through it. The second is with pain and suffering on a detour path (which will only get you back to the beginning, so that you can be present and experience your stuff as you work through it). Instead of looking for a distraction, be with whatever it is you have today.

Chapter 15

I AM NOT ME

When there is lack of congruence in our lives, there is a very big difference between who we think we are versus the truth of who we are. I am not my thoughts or the clothes I wear or the car I drive. These are all expressions of self, but they do not define me. I am no more than you and you are no more than me. The essence of people with university degrees is no different from the uneducated, and the rich are no different from the poor. These divisions and definitions are self-created.

The more layers of superficial identity into which we buy, the further we stray from ourselves. I am not me. I am a being that exists in a body and I am aligned to the universe. I only exist by virtue of the existence of everything else. All beings and matter around us are us. The apple cannot be anything other than a product of the tree it grows on. The essence of the tree lives in the apple; it cannot be any other way. This is universal truth and it is the core of everything. Nothing anywhere or anytime will ever change the core of your being. You are identical to every other manifestation of existence; whether static, alive or invisible. Any thoughts you have about yourself are merely subjective judgements. Whatever you think about yourself does not change your source core.

Our thoughts are creative because they are precursors to actions. Actions are causes which create effect. The events in our lives are either causes or effects, though the distinction is irrelevant: what is, is. While the experiences and events of our lives are monumental, they will never alter the very definite constitution of our being. We remain the beings that we are, just with layers that are created by our interpretation of the events of our lives.

All that vacillates in your world are the stories you tell yourself and believe.

When we stop engaging in the constant battle to figure things out and we no longer chase distractions, we return to source and find the things that we love; the things that nourish our essence. We feel good, wholesome, cherished and blessed. No fatigue, no stress and no undue pressure will be found. Instead: simple pleasures and abounding joy.

Chapter 16

HOPE IS HOPELESS

Hope will get you nowhere. Belief will get you everywhere.

Sometimes the fantasy of the 'next' seems so far removed from possibility that we frame it in an even more distant place called 'hope'.

One day we see that the distance between our hope-life and our now-life is so great that it's hopeless, so we begin to sabotage the fantasy. We'd rather destroy the game than lose. We start with behaviors that don't serve us. We begin to find ways to numb the pain of the now. This often manifests as self-destructive behavior such as substance, food or relationship abuse. We avoid pain at all costs; yet avoidance is the origin of pain and will be the cause of further pain in the next moment. The cycle repeats.

Hope becomes a disguised way of saying hopeless. Our subconscious minds believe that hope actually equates to not achieving the intention, and our thoughts ultimately create our experiences.

When we become aware that what we want is already in this moment, regardless of the circumstance, then we take responsibility for things being as they are and allow ourselves to be present without criticism, deferment or panic.

Why do the mansion, the sports car and the fairy tale love story have to be in our lives before we believe that we can relax into the moment? Our subconscious mind is aware that we aren't experiencing our self-created fantastical life, which in turn creates an atmosphere of subtle, subconscious disappointment. This is a travesty of reality. After all, we are only creating these wants so that we can feel a particular way. We experience the same amount of a particular emotion whether we are driving a sports car or a sedan. The perceived difference is just a story we tell ourselves.

The pursuit of fantasy is only in response to a desire for certain emotions. The same joy will permeate your life when you get to your holiday whether you got there in a sweaty raincoat or an air-conditioned luxury bus. The same joy will be experienced whether your holiday is on top of a mountain or in your buddy's back yard in a tent. Being in the now is about experiencing the moment as it is – no thoughts, no judgement, no interpretation – just presence.

There is nothing wrong with dreaming. It is these distractions from the now that allow us to find space in the present. When those split-seconds of make-believe evaporate, we often find the now tolerable.

I came to realize that I didn't actually want to be somewhere else. I wanted to be here, now, but on my terms, which included less pain. A psychologist or doctor can't propel you into a different place; they can only help you be comfortable with where you are.

Looking forward to something is usually far more exciting than actually achieving it. Wanting a different reality is only an exercise in deferment of joy. All joy is now. All happiness is now. Everything you desire is already here – squeeze the moment and feel this to be true.

Only wholesome intention will manifest results; hope without empowerment evaporates our power and suspends the process of positive creation by placating the ego instead.

Choose to live with intention rather than hope.

Chapter 17

TRAFFIC LIGHTS

Look closely at the things around you as you move through the world. Notice the traffic lights as you drive. Notice that some days all the traffic lights are green and other days they are red. Take note of your thoughts when the traffic lights are red.

Green traffic lights are synonymous with your integrity. When you see green traffic lights, keep thinking what you are thinking and keep doing what you are doing. Green traffic lights are indicative that you are on the correct path. When you see red traffic lights, it's a perfect opportunity to evaluate your thoughts. Red Traffic lights indicate that you may need to reconsider.

Have you ever noticed how traffic lights are red when you are late, slowing you down further? If you call ahead and let people know that you are going to be late, you will get back into integrity and the traffic lights will start turning green. When we continue to negotiate with ourselves, attempting to justify that we'll only be a few minutes late – when we know that it will be 15 or 20 minutes, we keep breaking the integrity cycle; thus creating more red traffic lights.

Listen to your universe. When the metaphorical (and literal) traffic lights in your life are green, go on. These are green traffic light days.

Red traffic light days are easy to change. Your thoughts create your experiences and the color of the traffic lights is no different. Change your thoughts. The traffic lights will change to reflect this and the day will unfold in a positive way.

Green traffic lights are indicative that you are on the correct path. Things will work in your world and opportunities will manifest. Joy will flow and all will feel right.

Red traffic lights are informative that you may be persisting with an avenue that is not the best for you. If something didn't work the first or second time, it's unlikely to work the third time.

If at first you don't succeed it doesn't always mean that the path is wrong, it may mean that the timing is wrong or an aspect of the path is not perfect. Simply flow with what is working. There are many paths in your life that will work – but if you hold your gaze on the doors that won't open, you have no ability to see other opportunities.

As the tumor shrunk day by day, I knew that it would eventually dissolve completely. I kept coming back to the memory of the day that I had given up fighting. I had surrendered to the outcome being whatever it would be. If that meant surgery with a dubious prognosis, then so be it. That was my lesson; to let go and trust the process of my life, knowing that ultimately I had very little control of what was already there, yet complete control of how I would interpret it, imbibe or fight going forward. I used to think I was 100% in control of the environment surrounding my life. On that day I realized that the environment had nothing to do with my life, and that the circumstances and events in my life were not me. They didn't define me. They were external. I was who I was - with a physical obstacle, a mountain to climb and a path to find.

Chapter 18

FEAR OF THE FEAR

You cannot be in fear if you are present in the moment. Fear comes from self-created future stories of usually improbable situations with unlikely outcomes. Right here, right now, you are safe. Fear is a future-based emotion.

In my early twenties, living in Africa and travelling regularly to Mauritius, which is an island a few hours east by airplane, I discovered snorkeling. I would float for hours watching the incredible habitat below. It was a natural progression to learn to SCUBA so that I could venture into the depths below and see more of the aquatic world.

The idea of having 60 feet of water above me excited me, but a sharp reality hit home on the first boat ride into the middle of the ocean. I started to worry about what would happen if something went wrong down there. What if my air stopped? What if I couldn't get my buoyancy right? What if I couldn't see? What if...

This fear was not based on anything real. It was based on my not having been able to see in murky water during one training dive, learning what to do if my air stopped in class and the general knowledge that getting buoyancy right as a new diver was difficult.

I was fine when I couldn't see during the training dive. I dealt with it. Although I was uncomfortable, I wasn't scared. I knew what to do if my air stopped and I knew I'd figure out the buoyancy thing, but that didn't stop me from worrying about what would happen if any of those things went wrong.

A lot of the time, the things that scare us are not the things of which we are afraid. I'm not saying that things that scare us aren't scary, I'm saying that being scared of them doesn't necessarily have much to do with the things themselves, but rather our fear of being scared.

I realized that actually I was scared of being scared.

Being scared of being scared or the *fear of the fear* is the root cause of fear. It's the exponential driver that takes a split second idea of something and catapults it into an avalanche reaction. But it's the fear of the avalanche that we fear most.

The worst kind of fear you can have is the fear of the fear. It's unnecessary and easily avoidable. Once you know that, you can eliminate that component out of the fear reaction equation and reduce anxiety.

Fear is the opposite of love.

Chapter 19

TIMING

It took just over four months for the tumor to dissolve. The radiologists were dumbfounded at each milestone. Some listened intently, stunned at how this could be happening and analyzing it in the medical context. How was it possible that meditation, visualization, yoga and some vegetable juice could have anything to do with it? One doctor demanded to know what medication I was taking, because he had never heard of any drug that could do this – but obviously there was one!

I really didn't need to have the last MRI, I knew the tumor was gone. The tumor and I had made peace a few days earlier – there was no doubt in my mind that it was gone.

Longing for the fire of North America, I moved from South Africa. I stumbled into an arbitrary studio one day near my apartment. I had a strong yoga practice and was excited to take a class in Vancouver, one of the world's yoga meccas. The class was packed full. I ended up squashed up against the wall with my life flashing before my eyes a few times during that class. I was somewhat disillusioned because it was a really difficult class and I doubted the likelihood that my body would ever be able to do any of those things.

My back was still tender, and even though the tumor was finally gone there was still a lot of residual aching and discomfort.

That night I wondered where my path was leading. I realized it really didn't matter; I completely trusted the process of life. Wherever I ended up would be wonderful. When we understand that we never really end up anywhere, life is fluid and dynamic.

It turned out that the teacher of this class would become my yoga mentor, and I would learn from her for years.

I've had other things spark in places and at times when I did not expect anything. This is how trust and the universe work; not with premeditated desire, but with opportunistic reward for showing up and shining alive.

I once drove across town at 6am to attend one of those business incubator meetings where people from different industries meet and promote each other. I was thinking that I ought to get another IT company going in my new city, because how else was I to survive? While I thoroughly enjoy computer work, it just didn't feel right that morning. I wondered why I was doing something that didn't feel right.

Months later, I drove the same road at the same time to take morning yoga classes with my teacher. I learned that sometimes the road feels wrong, but it's not always about the road or how you traverse it, it's about when you travel it - and why.

Maybe something in your life is the right thing at the wrong time.

If something doesn't work at a particular time, it may work at another time. That doesn't mean you keep doing the same thing in the same way at different times and avoid listening to your universe. If something doesn't work at a particular time in a particular way, test it at another time. If that doesn't work either, perhaps it's time to let it go.

Chapter 20

DESTINATIONS

There is always a destination. It is imperative to want to be where you are going, as opposed to not wanting to be where you are. The motivation for moving must be about where you will soon be as opposed to leaving where you are. This is the difference between proactivity and reactivity. While it may feel proactive to leave a stagnant place – it is only so if you want to be where you are going. This is why proactivity can fail.

Ultimately there are no specific destinations; only presence in the now. By referring to a path, we imply a beginning and an end. This linear thinking is a human characteristic and naturally how we operate. Yet there is never a true end or beginning. This moment is all there is.

The destination is always ahead of you; it's always there to be found.

Reaching the destination is the most unimportant part.

Chapter 21

HOOKS

Every person and situation you see is a reflection of yourself peering back at you. Whether it's happy reaction or uncomfortable prodding, it's all you. When we create stories about our lives and how we want them to be, we often fall into traps called hooks. Biting hooks is inevitable. However, if we are aware that we are doing this, it helps put things in perspective. When you know that you are reacting to something because that's what you always do, this awareness interrupts the automatic reaction and calms the situation. After all, everything is just a subjective reaction to what is. Either we see things this way or we see things that way. Either way, it simply is what it is.

How do we stop reacting to our stories? Or, how do we stop creating these stories? The answer is that we can't. However, there are spaces you can find by being still and experiencing the moment as is, without judgement and need to change. These places are found in meditation, on a yoga mat, martial arts, dancing and the like. The more time you spend in pursuit of these practices, the less your stories will mean, and the less reactionary you will be. Each day will become less and less difficult and more and more joyous. Give yourself permission to sit with whatever it is. Don't fight to get out of it - just be.

Life doesn't have to be one drama after the next. Letting go of your agenda regarding how other people's lives should look is freeing. You are not responsible for other people's behavior. You are responsible for being present in this particular space at this particular time and you are wholly responsible for your interpretation of the experience. How and why you ended up in a particular situation is irrelevant. You are already there.

Each being has its own agenda. The sooner you realize that your interpretation of the behavior and action around you is your only responsibility, the sooner you stop blaming yourself and the situation or person.

Once you are in an experience, the most powerful tool you have is choice. Choice empowers you to react to your interpretation of others' behavior or to accept that you have no control of other people and instead soften your shoulders in calm realization of this simple truth.

You are born, you live, you die.

A bus could hit you tomorrow or you could win the lottery. How true will your story be tomorrow?

Chapter 22

DIFFICULT SITUATIONS

When we release judgement and accept that there is no blame, no fault and that nothing was ever other than exactly what it was – then we are free to abandon hindsight and look back with perspective. We can awaken to see how situations evolved in the perfect space and time.

When we see that things are as they are; were as they were and will be as they will be, then we can release the stress of worrying. Worrying about the future is an exercise in futility. It is as much of a disservice to yourself as is dwelling in the past. You can't change anything by worrying about it or replaying it in your mind. All you will do is create negativity around the situation which will bring about the less desired outcome.

The more energy you expend on something the more reaction you will experience from it. Working hard will result in proportionate reward, whether in the direction of joy or suffering. The response to an experience and the immersion of yourself in "what is," as opposed to "what could be" or "what should be" is the measure of presence in your life. The ultimate gratitude is to ratify the moment by honoring it, not beleaguering it.

If we find that things are not manifesting how we expect them to, we can fight them or we can choose to surrender. We can accept that things are going to manifest how they do, when they do and perfectly. Everything is always for the greater good.

If we accept the events of our lives at face value, then we are free to take responsibility for all parts of our life. When we negotiate with the memories of the past, we find ourselves entertaining thoughts of blame, denial and renunciation. If we refuse to accept the events of the past exactly as they were, then we cannot exist fully in this moment.

It is often easier to make someone or something else responsible for the way we feel. Rather than owning the emotions that may be present in our lives at a particular time, we shift the responsibility elsewhere, giving our power away.

When we find fault in each other and blame others for supposedly causing our pain, we lose control over what's ours. We no longer simply feel the way we feel. Instead, we feel this way because of some circumstance or person. There is a shift away from experiencing our emotions. We give away experiences that are occurring for our growth and healing. We then miss the lesson, and we miss being able to help anyone else grow and heal because we are blinded by emotion. If we were to describe this it would sound like: "I am a helpless being, giving all my power away to you. I allow you to dictate my emotional responses to the events that you caused in my life. It's all your fault."

Somehow allowing our minds to assign responsibility to the other person makes us feel better. It's easier to blame someone else and make them wrong so that we can be right. Yet it doesn't change the past. Nothing can.

Chapter 23

ANGER

Anger is a power trip. You may feel that you have lost control of a situation, and in order to get some power back, you ignite your anger. You get louder and perceive yourself to be more powerful in doing so. You make something or someone else wrong so you can be right. If that means screaming and shouting, then that's what you do to appease yourself.

Of course anger is sometimes necessary, but it is important to be aware that it is a primal survival response and not an intelligent emotion born of love and trust.

Whatever you perceive love to be and however you choose to apply the action of loving, it all begins with the self. You've heard this a thousand times before. You can't hurt another human being without hurting yourself. You can't love another without simultaneously loving yourself. It's the same thing.

Chapter 24

GUT FEELING

When something doesn't feel right, it's not.

Trust yourself.

Basic survival instinct is deeply ingrained in every part of our being. We are wary of dangerous or uncomfortable situations and equipped to detect anything that threatens us.

We are able to recognize hazards, but are not as skilled at identifying safety.

This means that we often don't recognize positive situations. They can be clouded by the influence of our fear detection systems, which may invalidate our gut feelings when they tell us something could be good. How often do we allow risk and fear to prevent us from embracing that which we know to be beneficial?

Alternately, the ego's yearning for happy outcomes tends to minimize the validity of our fears, which in turn leads us into situations that may not serve us.

It's much easier to get into situations than it is to get out of them. Wanting something so badly that we ignore signs of danger only leads to destruction. Nothing good will ever come of talking yourself into something that doesn't feel right. As long as there is something in you causing hesitation, it's not right. Don't do it.

This is not to say you shouldn't listen to green traffic lights. If every single traffic light is green, keep walking that path. If there are messages to be received, they will appear at the right time to temper the travel.

Chapter 25

REGRET

Regret is only ever about invalidation. The content is irrelevant. Suffering always arises out of pain. Pain develops out of conflict or invalidation in the physical, emotional or spiritual arena.

Pain is always a messenger and ignoring it only increases its intensity. Resistance is misdirected persistence. The length and intensity of pain that you experience is directly proportional to your resistance of a situation.

The way you define the difference between your perception of your life and the life that your ego thinks you should be living is the foundation of regret. If you are experiencing regret, you are not present in the moment. Regret is something we use to justify the disappointments of the past. It's just thought created by entertaining the 'should haves', 'could haves' or 'might haves' in your life.

We often allow emotional pain to continue because there is some payoff. Apparently it feels good to feel bad. It's so easy to fall into negativity. Rather than having to compete with someone or something happy, we may choose to compare degrees of misery - as long as the next person is worse off.

We play the 'who is worse off' game. In order to win, we must sabotage ourselves and create negativity. We feel that we are worse off than the compared situation and then we get to wallow in a 'woe is me' feeling. Doing this makes any glimmer of happiness thereafter feel like a rainbow. I call this the differential of happiness.

Things were as they were. The past is done and nothing can change what was. As long as you keep your gaze behind you, you will not see what's in front of you.

Only when you surrender to the disappointment and let go of what may have been, can you be fully present in your now-life.

Be mindful of the words 'should', 'must' and 'have to' when referring to the future.

When our ego tells us that our opinion about something should be negative, this is when we enable the process of regret perception.

Most importantly, if you are hurting yourself – you are hurting someone else, whether in the direct situation that will cause your pain or from the ensuing fallout. Do we really mean to inflict harm on others? Will others experience the terrible things we wish for them, or will our negativity only produce a garden of weeds inside of us? When we realize that we are the other person and that everything that we want for another is actually what we wish for ourselves, we are able to reduce the pain and regret cycle in our lives.

When we nurture the world around us with abundant love and care, our lives become a much richer place in which to exist.

If you are unsure about whether to do something or not, ask yourself if you're hurting anyone or anything by doing it.

Then ask yourself: When tomorrow comes, will you be able to live with the repercussions of the decisions you make today?

If you can live with the consequences – go for it. If you know that you'll have regrets – don't.

Chapter 26

GUILT IS EXPENSIVE

Emotionally supporting thoughts of guilt is a draining and damaging pastime. It is likely that the action you know you must take to dissolve the guilt will give you freedom. Being honest with people from whom you are withholding truth is cathartic.

Releasing guilty energy by living truthfully will end the pain and fear in many other areas of your life. Guilt is a completely unnecessary emotion. It is a learned behavior and its purpose is to help us avoid feeling the pain of the truth. In fact there is no pain in truth. It is our 'stories' that pull us into the concept of guilt, and only our fear of the fear of pain keeps us there.

Chapter 27

ACCEPTANCE

When things don't work out as you want them to, accept that things are not working out as you want them to. If your intention is good and wholesome and part or all of it is to be of service to others, then overall good will prevail.

You are not in control. Our ego thinks we have it right when we will something to happen and it does. Yet all that happened was that we aligned with the universal energy that is present anyway. We became aware of it and congruent with it and then invited it to happen without resistance.

When things go wrong in your life, you may be the catalyst for things going right in someone else's life. Accept that you are being of service without knowing how or why.

Maybe your car stalling on the freeway prevented a massive accident a few miles behind. Life tends to a place of most benefit for all beings – it just may not seem this way to our egotistical mind at times.

Being of service is not about selfless existence, it's about accepting responsibility for your portion of the circumstances and doing something about it.

Chapter 28

THE BOW WAVE

When a boat navigates through the water, wake trails behind it. Wake is created as a consequence of the boat passing through the water. Similarly there exists a bow wave in front of the boat – the effect of the boat on the water in front of it – although the boat has not yet reached that point in the water. The same applies to you. The next event in your life is influenced by your current thoughts and actions.

The boat's next position is determined by 'the current moment – the current now'. The circumstances in 'the current now' are a result of past situations. The direction in which we choose to point the boat is a result of our emotional reactions to the past and our perception of what we think we want the future to be.

Your current experience was crafted by your thoughts a moment ago.

Everything in life is in process. One cannot describe oneself as walking without implying that the next event will also be walking. We cannot isolate the current event from the next event. Even if power to the boat is cut and the boat slows, the bow wave in front of it will change to reflect that event. Boats can't stop suddenly. The next event in your life is going to happen, whether you accept it or resist it.

You can't change your boat's direction unless you are on the boat. You can't navigate your life unless you are being honest with yourself.

The experiences that occur in your life are a result of your choices. The wake behind you is a result of past experience. The bow wave in front of you is impending experience, which is created from your current and past thoughts.

Thoughts and decisions put power to the boat to go forward, stop, turn left or turn right. Life can't go backward– it is a journey forward. We wastefully spend time and energy in the past, yet we can't change what was. When your life is not moving ahead it may feel stagnant and still, but it's never going backward.

You are driving the boat, and in front of you, the bow wave of impending experience is being created.

Chapter 29

BEACONS

Each day you will encounter new people on your path. These complete strangers who ordinarily pass by are your beacons.

If you want to know who you are, look at the people in your life. Each situation in your life will have a different set of people present and this will represent the status of your thoughts. All of your characteristics are mirrored back at you via the people who are in your space at a particular moment. If there are many people in the space, each person will characterize a more finite aspect of you. If there are only a few people present, there will be broader, less defined traits of yourself being mirrored back at you.

When you are reactive to a situation, person or group of people this indicates that the thing to which you are reacting is present inside of you and is being mirrored. This is different to categorizing yourself as being similar to the people around you by labeling yourself with the same sticker. For example, everybody is able to experience the emotion of anger. If you are in a group of people that are angry, it does not define you as an angry person, unless you are also angry. Instead it may evoke another emotion that is reactive to the angry people. This is your mirror.

People come and go as the seasons change and the world evolves. Nothing is forever. You'll never get to the finish line in this life, because there is no beginning or end. There is no goal or destination, no purpose or checklist to achieve. The purpose of this life is to learn, grow and love: to become aware that you are the other person and every other being on the planet. There is no set of circumstances that will be achieved once you master the various aspects of existence, because the end game doesn't exist. You cannot win or lose, fail or succeed in this life. All you can achieve is disconnection from ego and resonance with truth and the universe.

Like attracts like. Happy spaces attract happy people. Happy people attract more happy people. Happy people resonate to create a healing mechanism that dissolves sadness. Joy will always overwhelm sadness, because joy resonates at a higher frequency and is powerful. The very essence of life is joy-based. Practicing joy is a reconnection to the core of existence.

If a person possesses an attribute that annoys you, this is your stuff. If someone is pushing your buttons, be grateful that you have created the perfect person to mirror you. You are not the victim. You are in fact the instigator. It is an opportunity for you to grow. Ironically, it is the person who is annoying you that will benefit most. The annoyer is unable to annoy themselves, so they unconsciously seek out a person who will point out the areas in their life that need healing. If you care enough about that person, you will be unable to resist the invitation to heal with them.

The typical response in a challenging situation is to depart from the game, yet the mechanism of growth is to get conscious, be totally present in the moment, feel the emotions and deal with them.

Usually the people who irritate us are the people who are closest to us, and we are unable to simply destroy the game and leave. Instead we can choose to be mindful, not making the other person wrong, and acknowledge that we created the presence of this person in our lives to heal us. In return we can be of service to this person by being a catalyst to initiating healing in their life.

The people who appear in your life and test you care enough about you to reflect your lessons back at you. It is in these moments of utter frustration, anger and disbelief that you must especially send love to the people who are mirroring your hidden emotions. Instead of reacting to your own traits being demonstrated by others and ultimately reacting to yourself, send love outward.

By empowering our own healing, we are automatically healing the next person. This occurs as a symbiotic exchange. The other person created you in their life as much as you created them in your life.

An example: You share a living space with a person who incessantly leaves cupboard doors open, which drives you nuts. The short answer is that you need to learn to live with open cupboards, but more importantly the other person needs to learn to close the cupboard doors.

If you are not honest with the people in your life you are doing them a disservice. If you go through life out of congruence and out of integrity, thinking one thing and saying another, not only does it hurt you, it hurts others. If you choose to live in a space of congruent truth, this will manifest people of equal truth.

Noticing the patience of an elephant tells you that you are patient. Recognizing the beauty in a flower tells you that you are beautiful. Whatever you see in something else is already in you.

When you see the light in someone else, you are seeing your inner star, your own light reflected back at you. The more honest your connection with another, the more you will see of yourself. If you will not see the light in another, it usually means that you are refusing to look at your own reflection or denying the bright light emanating from you.

Not only do all people in our lives possess the qualities that we already have in ourselves, but they are also the qualities that require rekindling. We create people in our lives to satisfy the complex process of growth and forgiveness.

If you see unbounding love, abundant care and light in someone else, remind yourself that if it was not in you, you would not recognize it.

If you feel that your life could use more cheer, place yourself alongside joyous people and you will shift – it is inevitable. I've yet to find a place more joyous than the yoga mat – it's where my joy originates.

As a yoga teacher, I have learned that being a mirror to my students is kind, but it's not the ultimate service I can deliver.

In regular relationships with people to whom we are close, being the mirror means taking on the interaction and engaging. This is good.

In order to be totally present for all my students, I realized that I could not be an effective mirror for everyone - let alone one person - and teach at the same time.

That evolved into my understanding that being a true teacher meant holding the mirror up for my students to see themselves reflected, and specifically not being the mirror myself. Just like being a friend who offers no advice, and only ever reflects back everything that is said - but without words.

Chapter 30

TEACHING YOGA

Whatever draws people to yoga is unlikely to be what keeps them there. When I stumbled upon yoga it simply felt good. I didn't know anything about anything, except that more traffic lights were green more of the time on the drive home.

I can say for certain that if you take it a step further and start doing some training and even become a teacher, it's no longer up to you. Yoga chooses you. And by yoga I mean the lifestyle of physical congruence and integrity; the flow with universal energy and not against it.

I took a yoga teacher training course, and despite a lot of internal resistance and uncertainty, I began to teach two months later. After thousands of additional hours of training, courses, meditation and a deeper understanding, I was also certified as a prenatal yoga instructor, and finally, a teacher trainer. I was now able to instruct and develop teachers. As my classes got bigger, I started to hear from more and more students about how this practice was changing their lives, and how they were healing, growing and shining.

Teaching yoga has something, but not much, to do with the teacher. We are humble beings in service to others, passing on a gift while we facilitate an experience. Nothing makes this clearer to me than the words that come out of my mouth when I am teaching. They are not planned, rehearsed or even known to me most of the time. Often I stop and think – "what did I just say? Could someone say that to me? It sounded like something I should hear".

Whether it's teaching yoga, college or life, we all teach what we need to learn.

Each person is a teacher and has a skill or message to pass on for the greater good of all. What is it that you teach?

Chapter 31

IT'S JUST AN ICE CREAM.
IT'S NOT FOREVER.

Our human nature is to want to have things forever. We become attached to ideas, people and places. We want to freeze them in time. A fair amount of our self-inflicted suffering comes from the knowledge that we don't have the power to sustain anything forever. When we realize that something isn't sustainable, we immediately set out to remedy that. When we find the imminent reasons why it can't be sustainable, we start negotiating with the current situation in an attempt to change the future. This causes anxiety and triggers suffering in our lives.

When we eat wonderful tasty food, our brains are in conflict. On the one hand the neural pathways are alight and stimulated by the delicious food, and on the other, our subconscious knowledge is that this meal will end. So we learn to savor the food slowly. Making the moment everything that it can be right now is what matters. No matter how much we want to make it last forever, it won't.

We sometimes write off situations because we don't think they will last beyond tomorrow. We destroy the game before we even make the first move. Live your life. Please don't miss out on being in your now-life based on what you think tomorrow may not be. Never write off a seemingly impossible situation until you contribute your unique talent to it. That's tantamount to giving up on a dehydrated plant before you water it. What may seem unachievable could become reality tomorrow based on a variable you never expected.

If you proceed with full integrity, intention and trust, who's to say that something extraordinary won't happen?

Don't give up before you start. Do the best you can, and always trust the process of your life.

Chapter 32

TRYING

To try is not to do. Trying to do something will render a result similar to that of not doing anything. The word try implies that you will take actions leading to a potential result, but you don't expect to succeed. Announcing that you are 'trying' is simply a way of preparing for your expected failure or your unexpected success.

If you truly believed that you could not succeed at something, you wouldn't even attempt it. It only requires a glimmer of belief in your success for you to initiate an action in an unknown direction. We often mistakenly call this *trying*, when in fact it is proactively *doing*.

We either do or we don't. Trying is not half way between starting and finishing. To try is to sit on the start line.

Entertaining the idea of not succeeding in an area in which you believe you have capability is nothing more than an invalidation of yourself. Whether you perceive success or not is irrelevant. What matters is how much you believe in yourself and how much you trust the process to provide the perfect result.

Making the announcement that you will try to hit a home run only introduces the idea that failure is a possibility. Including the option of failure in your language influences the likelihood of completely succeeding. If you don't hit the home run, you are not going to be any more justified in not succeeding by announcing that you tried. Entertaining the option of failure is a disservice to yourself. If you do something and don't succeed, it is simply a lack of success - it is not failure. The only failure is not beginning in the first place.

Everything is for the good. No matter what, no matter how, no matter the tremendous price we sometimes pay – everything is ultimately for the good.

Chapter 33

LIFE IS IMPORTANT, BUT IT'S NOT SERIOUS

Treat your life with the respect and reverence it deserves. Honor yourself, honor your brothers and sisters, be a shining light of joy. But please don't take yourself seriously.

The world can be a simple, happy place. Yes, there are crazy things in this world, but how you exist among all of this is your choice. It determines how much service you can be to yourself and to love. Taking your life so seriously that you squeeze the joy out of everything will only make for a lifetime in which even the happy moments are shrouded in a cloud of doom. Every time you force the love out of life, you hurt the people around you. Every time you suffer, you cause the people around you to suffer.

Life is not about beating the next person in order to survive, but about looking out for each other.

How would it be if you were responsible for everyone else's success instead of your own? That would mean that other people were responsible for your success. What if you couldn't run the race yourself, but instead your success depended on your brother? How would it be if your success was based on everyone else's victory instead of on your own ability?

Our survival, happiness and conscious presence depend entirely on each other. Alone we are meaningless; just snowflakes in the wind. Yet as part of the whole, we have infinite power. Love is the key. Love is everything. There is nothing else. Everything else comes from over-thinking, over-analyzing and being distracted from presence.

Chapter 34

LIFE, DEATH AND GRIEF

Live every moment of your life to the fullest. If you weren't supposed to, you wouldn't be alive or able to in the first place.

Fear of death is one of the most disempowering emotions. If you live in fear of death, your life will never be a full expression of your true potential. You are going to die at some point. It's just a question of when. When we realize that it doesn't matter when we are going to die, we see that life is for living. Life is not the absence of death; death is the absence of life.

Our few years of physicality are miniscule in the scheme of things.

Nothing ever dies; it changes form. Yes, the body gets old and people leave their bodies eventually. This is why you are not your body. You are you, within your body. Your body is an extension of your spirit and is present to enable you to experience your energy in a tangible way.

Because we are responsible for experiencing the events of our lives, we take responsibility for these experiences. They don't belong to anyone else. They are ours alone. Because this blip of time present on earth in physical form is so short, there is little time to mess around or take it too seriously.

When we pass, we exit the physical system and the world as we know it know, returning to presence in another realm. Because of our physical presence, we frame all understanding around physicality. It is very difficult for us to conceive that we are in all forms at all times and there are no definitive beginnings or ends.

When the karma and the lessons of this lifetime are complete, we leave our bodies and go back to the place from where we came. It is only in physicality that we sometimes choose to be alone. In spirit, in every moment, we are always together. The relationships you are experiencing as a human are small beginnings. We've met here to verbalize and work out a few things. We were never apart and we will never be apart. It is only our minds that perceive distance and separation, and this is where suffering originates.

Those we love are going to pass on. So are you. So am I. When will this happen? That's the variable. Our attachment to physicality creates suffering. When you become aware that you have created your fear of loved ones passing, then you will breathe some relief and the fear will dissolve. You will know that they are going to meet their ancestors and future family, and you will find peace in that knowledge.

You will meet loved ones in dreams and you will meet them when you pass. You will see them in your family to come, and you will laugh and cry together. You will see that life is short. It's important, but it's not so serious.

There is more to death than the reactive doctrine that we usually fall into. Of course you will experience grief. That's why you're here. Not to avoid pain, but to evolve from it.

Chapter 35

FAITH

Faith has nothing to do with anything external in your life. We don't need to have something tangible in which to have faith. Faith exists independent of the belief that something else extraordinary may or may not direct our lives. Faith is about letting the process of life be as it is and allowing it to unfold as it does, without interference or intellectual negotiation with our stories.

Faith is about knowing without having to justify our thoughts and beliefs. Faith is about letting go of all expectations with an unquestionable trust that whether we interfere or not, things will work out perfectly. Faith is about not questioning why, but having dedicated intention to the wholeness of our lives by living in congruence with ourselves and therefore existing with integrity.

You or I do not have any more right to anything than the next person. When we believe that having more than someone else makes us superior, this only demonstrates how little faith we have in ourselves.

There will always be people with more than you and people with less than you. There will always be rich and poor, sick and healthy and weak or strong. Yet, to each person their own strength is invisible when compared to that of someone stronger, and their weaknesses are greater than those to which they compare themselves. Comparison is thought (ego) that distracts us from our own path of internal faith.

Faith is about surrendering from our monkey mind, the stories we tell ourselves and the beliefs we create from those stories. Our stories are irrelevant because the way things are cannot be changed. Only the way we interpret the events of our lives and where we put our next foot is within our control. The closer we are to the source of our power, which is located within us, the more influence we have. The greater your congruence within yourself, and the greater your faith, the stronger your influence will be on the things around you and the greater your contribution to situations and events.

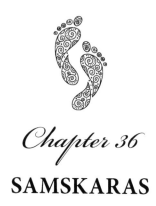

Chapter 36

SAMSKARAS

"Samskara" is Sanskrit for "habits"

How many times have you misplaced or lost something, and, convinced that it was in the place where you expected it, kept returning to that place to find it?

Why do we keep repeating the same actions and expect a different reaction?

What is universally true will always be, and no amount of "samskara" negotiation will change that. You can't plant a banana and expect an apple tree to grow.

If what you're looking for isn't where you think it should be, you may be looking for the wrong thing. Maybe what you're looking for is in a different place or maybe you're looking at the wrong time. Regardless of the reason, if something isn't where you think it should be, stop hitting your head against the wall trying to find it. If it's not there, move on.

You have to touch a hot pot on a stove to understand that doing so it isn't a good idea. No amount of being told not to touch something hot will stop a child from doing it. We learn through living. Setbacks and stumbling blocks are all clues to the secrets in the bigger scheme of where our lives will lead. There are no shortcuts. However, it is my belief that a yoga mat, a meditation cushion and a deliberate loving-kindness practice, combined with a life of congruence, integrity, truth and service, will expedite the process of living your true purpose. This will allow you to abandon samskaras and repetitive patterns of expectation.

Chapter 37

LOVE

The path is the path. We get to define our direction, but ultimately there is no destination. Whether you end up an astronaut, a businessperson, a yoga teacher or a holy leader — it doesn't matter. What you did is of no particular consequence once you are gone, but how you did it is everything. Maybe you touched lives in a beautiful way, maybe you caused children to smile, maybe you were a great teacher and saved the world from disease. If you made a big difference, you were present in your life. You weren't distracted or incongruent or out of integrity.

I don't refer to any particular religion or belief that you may have about where you came from. Ultimately we all come from the same place. How you choose to describe your doctrine is your choice. All the wisdom traditions believe in the same source, it's just interpreted with different lenses and over the years each has developed a set of community traditions. The life force within you is no different to that which is within me. Maybe we have different names for our beliefs. All roads lead to and come from the same place — LOVE.

Love is everything. It is the only way you can experience life. Life without love is impossible, yet we seek to cover up the love within so as not experience the essence of life. Love is not only good and easy. It is not just soft, happy experiences. Love is the sadness too. It is the pain and the difficulty. It is the obstacles and it is the road.

What will matter most after you are gone is how deep a connection you had to the shared experience of love.

Chapter 38

THE THREE PEOPLE CHALLENGE

Each day, it is our privilege to make a difference in the world. It is the small gestures in our lives that create the biggest shifts in the world. It is one of my favorite things to induce laughter or bring a smile to the lives of three complete strangers, with whom I ordinarily have no reason to interact, every day.

If you could do something that would bring laughter to thousands of people, would you do it? If you could alleviate another person's pain by simply smiling, would you? Would you risk being vulnerable for a split second and smile at the person passing by on the chance that it changes their life forever?

This challenge is specifically about smiling when you ordinarily wouldn't.

As you smile, you perpetuate good energy. If you smile at 3 strangers and they in turn smile at 3 strangers, who then smile at 3 strangers, in a matter of seconds you've influenced hundreds of people.

If you smile at 3 people every day, the whole world will be smiling all the time.

If you want to contribute to the world in a positive way, take this challenge. We don't need a license to spread positivity. We don't need permission. It's our birthright to be happy, to breathe and to love.

By smiling at 3 people each day, and an additional 3 for every smile you receive, you perpetuate the flow of joy. I promise you, your life will become easier, happier and lighter, by doing just this one thing; this one act of love.

I promise that if you choose to shine alive today – you will light up someone's life tomorrow.

Chapter 39

A SECOND CHANCE

I live with the repercussions of damage to my intervertebral disks that occurred during the tumor episode. The soft spongy disks normally keep the bones from grinding on each other and in my case the spaces are reduced. I'm not worried. Even though it may take years, each day my intention is that the disks are rebuilding, absorbing the nutrients they need to become plump and wholesome again.

There are days I wrap myself up into a pretzel in a yoga class and there are also days that walking is painful. But there is no longer any trace of the tumor, just a little of the memory it left behind to remind me to be present and not return to old thought patterns and old ideas, or to walk the path backwards. As intentional beings, we look forward and move forward, living with conviction and faith in our now-lives.

Chapter 40

SHINE ALIVE

No person has super-powers to heal others.

The healing reaction in my life didn't come from me. I was merely an open and receptive conduit, allowing universal energy and healing to permeate my body.

I did the work by preparing the landscape so that my body was receptive. I cleared the emotional blockages and opened my heart.

We often believe that there is someone or something out there that holds the ability to do our work or instigate our healing. Only we can do the work to make the space for this. We must trust the universe to do the rest.

There are many conduits and channels aligned with universal integrity. They are able to concentrate love and accelerate healing for others. You'll know them when you find them. Sometimes all it takes is a tree or an ocean or a pet. This doesn't mean that you need anyone or anything external to heal, just a partnership with the universe. If, however, you have the option to walk along your path with a healing entity, it's important to utilize that gift.

When I teach a yoga class, present a seminar or guide a meditation, I stand as a humble servant of the universe to facilitate the exchange of energy and wisdom. It is not me who offers the teachings. I'm there to articulate words and guide movement, which often elicits or initiates healing.

Why do I choose this path of service? Because for every piece of information I pass on, I learn something. Because I watch people's lives transform in ways that no one would believe. Because I know that there is hope for the world if we practice a lot of loving-kindness.

Or is it because I have no choice?

The truth is, this is just my path. I have very little control, but I have the luxury of being able to interpret the events of my life. There are green and red traffic lights all the time. There are messages and signals, tears and song. Yet all roads have lead to here; to my now-life. Not my yesterday-life or my tomorrow-life; my NOW-LIFE. It's enough to just be here now. I don't need to know what's next. I don't need to know how it all turns out. All I need to do is show up, right here, right now, with congruence and integrity, and with my feet facing forward.

There are no accidents.

Shine alive, my friend.